Desperate Executives

Forthcoming titles in the
Changing World of Work Series

Partnership and Organisational Change
by Dr John O'Dowd

The State of the Unions
edited by Dr Tim Hastings

Workplace Partnership in Practice:
Can Pluralism Produce Mutual Gains?
by Dr Tony Dobbins

Desperate Executives

A Story of Coaching, Change and Personal Growth

Dr Paul Mooney

The Liffey Press

≋ the
liffey
press

Published by
The Liffey Press
Ashbrook House, 10 Main Street
Raheny, Dublin 5, Ireland
www.theliffeypress.com

A catalogue record of this book is
available from the British Library.

ISBN 978-1-905785-39-1

Printed in the Republic of Ireland by Colour Books

National
College of
Ireland

The Changing World of Work Series

*T*he worlds of industrial relations (IR) and human resource management (HRM) are changing at a rapid rate. Through its involvement with adult learners over more than five decades, the National College of Ireland has been at the forefront in understanding and mapping these developments. Its reputation for providing relevant learning experiences and disseminating "best practice" has resulted in the acquisition of new skills for large numbers of IR/HRM professionals.

Through the Changing World of Work Series the National College of Ireland will be exploring the latest developments in the Irish workplace. The series will include an exploration of up-to-date themes around personal leadership, world-class management, the evolution of workplace partnerships, the state of trade unionism and managing change in both the private and public sectors.

This series seeks to address the central issues facing managers, workers and unions at a time when the boundaries of industrial relations and human resource management are being redrawn. The Changing World of Work Series will examine key research outputs and concepts in each area and outline the challenges which lie ahead.

About National College of Ireland

*F*or over 50 years, National College of Ireland has been a leading provider of graduates with the skills and knowledge to meet the existing and emerging needs of the Irish economy. Evolving with the changing employment landscape, the College has built an enviable reputation for excellence in education and for designing curriculum that is relevant to the workplace.

The College today is a not-for-profit, third-level education institution with a diverse student population. Reflecting the Jesuit value of social justice on which it was founded, National College of Ireland focuses on widening participation in higher education and on providing a student experience that allows individual potential to be fully realised.

Awknowledgements

While the characters portrayed in this book are fictional, they are a composite of real clients and presenting issues which I've had the privilege to work with. A debt of gratitude is due to the many clients who allowed me to work alongside them, as we both struggled through the issues which emerged.

In terms of basic concepts, they've come from so many different sources that it's impossible to acknowledge ownership. I suspect that some of the ideas are so old they were formulated by executive coaches working in caves! Several of the 'technical' concepts come from the general literature around counselling, psychotherapy and coaching. Working directly with executives over the past 25 years has also provided an insight into practical approaches that add value. As with all coaching work, the points made have also been shaped by my own life experience. Sometimes I've encountered clients with deeper, unresolved issues which needed more specialised support – and this book is not directed at that audience.

Sonya Goulding did the marathon typing (after the 28th draft, it got really easy). Anne Breakell, Linda Brunton, Liam Doherty, Deirdre Giblin, Tim Hastings, Niamh Imbusch, Emma Kytzia and Niall Saul read earlier versions of the text and suggested many useful changes. A huge thanks to each for the insights and the time given so generously. All remaining misquotations, errors and mistakes are my own.

All royalties from the sale of this book will be paid to the National College of Ireland.

Dr Paul Mooney
January 2008

The New Class: First Night Nerves

It was the same before every new class. A mixture of apprehension and excitement. Tonight was no different.

Mr Cheung went through his warm-up ritual, stretching each muscle group in turn, working from his feet upwards. The same routine he'd been shown by Wang Chee-Zou, all those years ago in Guangdong Province. Another lifetime. Turning his lifelong martial arts hobby into a business had been a masterstroke. Overnight he'd moved from being a mechanical engineer in a multinational construction company to running a workout studio. Executive Fitness in Sandymount, Dublin 4, was born.

The target market was well-defined and well-heeled. For a number of years overweight executives and bored housewives had been the staple diet. But then the fitness business changed. The stereotypical clients of those early days had become an eclectic mix of Dublin society, people seeking new leisure pursuits, looking for a break from the relentlessness of the 'Celtic Tiger'.

In ten years Mr Cheung had passed on his fitness skills to countless thousands of students. He'd discovered that an intensive, eight-week programme worked best. Payment up front (because, inevitably, some of the group would drop out of the classes).

They came for a myriad of reasons. Some to hone their physical strength. A small, but definite percentage wished to toughen themselves mentally. Others searched for an inner peace which had somehow eluded them. Losing a couple of inches to squeeze into a wedding dress or meeting a new partner was often the outward rationale to sign-up. However, Mr Cheung knew that uncovering the core reason which motivated clients to join was critical in bringing about lasting change.

Of course, the exercise itself was a benefit. The release of endorphins guaranteed a short-term buzz – an instant sweat-reward. But it didn't last and it wasn't enough. Clients needed something more, something sustainable. Mr Cheung saw himself as a sort of detective – helping clients to discover their 'true north' and charting a course towards this.

As he warmed up he wondered what tonight's class would bring. Exercises completed, he quickly logged onto www.blackjack.com. To Mr Cheung the internet did not represent real gambling. A small flutter would help ease the rigours of a new class. Tonight he would set a €100 bet limit. Tops. He made a silent promise that he'd stick to it.

Louise Gets Ready to Go

Across town, in a small two-bedroomed terraced house in Marino, Louise was thinking about her keep-fit resolution. According to the blurb, Dance-Boxing provided the cardiovascular workout of boxing with the 'flexercise' of a dance class. Good promise potential. Putting more time into her appearance was on the 'to do' list. These classes were an effort to do something constructive to address this.

Louise felt she needed the fitness class. Partly to get back in shape; mostly as time-out. Since her dad died (almost a year ago; it felt like yesterday) Louise had been looking after her mother. Louise's mother constantly bemoaned the fact that she was lonely. At some level Louise felt her mam might even secretly enjoy the widow status. It offered the leading role in a play called 'moaning', a licence to whinge without the stress of having to do anything about it. Executive Fitness would provide a Tuesday night escape, precious moments for Louise to invest in herself.

The negative thoughts about her mother, which intruded frequently, seemed disloyal. Louise knew a couple of people who had taken on the carer role with elderly parents. They seemed to be able to cope well enough (not just cope, some of them relished the role). Was she missing the sympathy gene?

Booking the fitness classes had been the first totally selfish thing Louise had done since her father passed on. It was liberating in an 'I'm doing this for me' kind of way. Tonight, the feelings about her mother were in full flow, partly fuelled by an earlier conversation ('Go ahead and look after yourself. Since your father left, there's just this awful loneliness. A whole life given to a husband and an only child. It was a mistake'). The rain outside was falling in sheets, adding to the gloom. A night for the gym.

Robbie Parks His Car

Robbie pulled his silver BMW 5 series into a free space at the end of a row. Executive Fitness's car park was tight. He didn't want someone chipping his metallic paintwork when opening their door. This exercise routine would fit neatly into his schedule. Monday and Thursday lunchtimes were solidly booked with racketball. Jogging on Wednesday and Friday; a full gym workout on Saturday. Sundays were kept free. His partner, Alan, would cook something at home – promised this weekend as a 'Mediterranean Surprise'. Typically, they would sleep and eat late.

Dance-Boxing sounded a bit nouveau but the instructor, Mr Cheung, got good press from colleagues in the International Financial Services Centre (IFSC) where Robbie worked, next door to the National College of Ireland. At 42, Robbie was increasingly aware of the need to keep fit. Combining fitness and flexibility seemed ideal. Maybe even a bit of fun.

The men's changing area was impressive. Teak wood and solid brass fittings. Robbie folded his trousers neatly and hung them alongside his Armani jacket. At 6'1" he was conscious of the first signs of middle-age spread. The exercise regime seemed to be holding back the tide – just about. He looked the part in a tracksuit purchased during a weekend trip to Genoa (Robbie and Alan didn't do package holidays). Those Italian men were stylish, he reminisced.

While he'd voluntarily signed up for this class, Robbie felt a slight tinge of unease – almost a premonition that something was about to change. A quick, satisfied glance in the full-length mirror, and then he made his way into the training area.

Getting to Know You, Getting to Know All About You

The first thing that struck Dan was how young the other people were. At 49 he was definitely the oldest in the room – 'almost grand-dad age'. His wife Joan had signed him up for the classes – a quirky Christmas gift he was still trying to figure out. The class was 7.00 pm until 9.00 pm. Written in large print on the brochure. No ambiguity. It was now precisely 7:07 according to Dan's watch and a younger, dark-haired guy just bounced into the room, late. No apology, nada. How inconsiderate, Dan thought.

The instructor seemed unperturbed, almost amused. Mr Cheung announced that he wanted each person to introduce themselves and state what they wanted to get out of the class. Dan was mortified. It was bad enough being the oldest in some new-age exercise class, without having to subject himself to the indignity of public speaking. His palms began to sweat. The guy who'd arrived late offered to go first.

'Hi, I'm Ed.'

'Hi, Ed' (collectively from the group). Dan said nothing.

'Now, where to start. Well, I work for a large manufacturing company – Performa. We make industrial products – shelving, storage, racking – boring stuff. My job is Purchasing Manager, putting the squeeze on all the tiny suppliers.'

Ed paused. 'Okay, that was a joke. You know the jokes are not working when you have to tell people, "hey, that was a joke".' The group nodded encouragement.

'Three kids. A six-year-old, a four-year-old and a six-month-old surprise.'

A couple of people smiled.

'I'm punching in long hours at work and not getting much sleep at home. So I figured this exercise class is going to be a doddle. Two hours a week off the treadmill. That's why I signed up for Executive Fatness'.

The group seemed a little uneasy – not quite sure how to react to Ed's exuberant style or whether another punch-line was going to be delivered.

'Thank you, Ed. I hope you find what you look for here.'

There was no acknowledgement or correction of Ed's mispronunciation of the Club's name. Mr Cheung's speech was so heavily accented, the group had to strain to understand the meaning. The session continued as each participant (nine in total) introduced themselves. Mr Cheung formally greeted each person in turn after they'd spoken. A couple of people were prominent.

Louise was a single woman living in Marino. She worked as a chemical engineer in a project management company. Robbie, a tall guy from Sandymount, had trained as a chartered accountant but was now a commodities trader in the Irish Financial Services Centre. Dan didn't mention what he did or where he lived, just the fact that he had two grown up kids and his wife booked the exercise class – without informing him in advance. Ed had a young family, combined with a pressurised job and just needed to escape. There were others in the group, but these were the people who stood out.

The introductions had eaten up almost an hour without a single exercise routine starting. The group were sitting in a circle, leaning back against the mirrored walls to get support. Mr Cheung maintained eye contact as he addressed them:

'My name Cheung Chen-Lou. Students call me Mr Cheung. I come from China, near to Hong Kong. You come here for variety of reason. Some you want physical fitness. Some maybe want to strengthen body against sickness. Some just try something new. My job is help you discover reason. This part of class is fitness for your mind. I am coach; you main player. Button for change your life is on inside. I help you find button. When you find, you become Chief Executive of your life.'

He paused for a moment before continuing. 'Why you want to change at all? You change because something bothering you. Or you want something to achieve. There no other reason to change. Now time for exercise. Stand up please and follow me.'

Mr Cheung began to demonstrate a simple movement with his right leg. 'Inside, then outside.' The participants copied the movement. 'Now, left side. Inside, then outside.'

Fifty minutes later the class ended. The group was exhausted, thankful that the introductions had eaten up so much time at the front-end. Dan had never felt so tired in his entire life. He was completely wiped, barely able to walk to the showers.

The Coffee Dock: One Week Later ...

A small cordoned area, just off the main entrance to Executive Fitness, was officially called the Juice Bar, but everyone referred to it as the Coffee Dock. While it was possible to buy a range of smoothies and multi-vitamin drinks, caffeine seemed to be the best-seller. After the second night's workout, a small group from the class ended up going there.

'Okay, anyone for a skinny decaf cappuccino? That can't be bad for you.' Ed was in boisterous form and was first up to buy the drinks. Louise ordered a cappuccino, Dan a regular black coffee and Robbie opted for juice. Once they'd settled down with the drinks, Louise kicked off the conversation.

'Last Wednesday, the day after our first class, I was exhausted. I'd pains in places where I didn't know I had muscles.'

'You are probably out of shape,' Dan suggested, unhelpfully.

'Possibly,' Louise said.

Ed settled back in his seat, balancing a mug of coffee and an oversized apple Danish. 'Life is your lobster,' Ed remarked as he tucked into a mouthful of cake.

'Your oyster,' Dan corrected.

'I was being ironic – but I don't suppose you do irony, do you Dan?'

'Hey guys. Let's re-start the clock. Thank you for the coffee Ed.' Louise raised her cup in a gesture of thanks, trying to ease the tension.

'How do you feel the class is going Dan?' she asked.

'Okay, I guess. It's a bit more physical than

expected but that's okay. I'm just not 100 per cent sold on the philosophy lesson, the "fitness for your mind" bit.'

'It's not quite what you expected?' Robbie asked.

'Exactly. After the first week, I almost wasn't going to come back. At my age you lose a bit of flexibility. I'm getting too old for all this jumping around.'

'How old are you anyway?' Ed asked bluntly.

'Ed, did you miss the semester on subtlety?' Louise's tone was disapproving.

'I'm 49, it's not a state secret.' Dan seemed nonplussed about revealing his age.

'Well 49 is not that old. My dad is 66.'

'Thanks for the vote of confidence, Robbie, but that's exactly my point. Your *dad* is 66. To be honest, I felt a little bit out of my depth the first night with everyone else being so young and all.'

'What age do you think Mr Cheung is?' Louise asked.

'I don't really know. Difficult to say. Late 50's, perhaps?'

'Well, there you go. Age is a state of mind. If you think you're old, you are old. And vice versa.'

Louise was smiling, satisfied she'd killed off the 'too old' argument.

'I don't buy the mind-over-matter stuff. Just

because you think you're the CEO of your life, you don't actually have more control over what happens to you. It's not clever, it's naïve,' Ed countered.

'I'm not sure I get the "CEO of your own life" either. I don't want to sound negative but some people end up with bad health, their kids get sick or whatever. You can't write the script,' Dan agreed with Ed.

'Yeah, it's a neat idea, but it's bullshit.' Ed had become more forceful on the point.

Robbie looked thoughtful, as if he was forming a sentence in his mind. 'I'm not suggesting that shit doesn't happen. However, while you can't control what happens, you can dictate your response. I think that's what Mr Cheung meant when he spoke about being the CEO of your own life.'

'Maybe with the benefit of a Jesuit education I could come up with similar logic. You're not in control, but you are in control? Is that your thesis?'

'I'm not trying to convince you, Ed. It's something I'm wrestling with myself.' It was spoken with a sincerity which made Robbie seem very real.

'What do you think Louise?' Robbie raised his eyebrows, waiting on her answer.

'Sort of similar initial take on it. I joined to

get fit, not for counselling. But during the week I found myself mulling over a couple of things that Mr Cheung said. It must have struck a chord, somewhere.'

'For instance?'

'Well the idea that you are the Chief Executive of your own life was particularly useful.'

'What's so novel about that?' Ed shrugged. 'It's been around forever.'

'Maybe so. But I'm not big on novelty. It's not whether an idea is new or old, but whether it's right or wrong.'

'The Chief Executive of your own life idea struck a chord?' Robbie reflected back.

'Well, and this might be getting a bit deep, it did resonate. Some other time I will bore you guys with the details.'

'You could *never* be boring,' Ed suggested. The remark was somewhat ambiguous and the group was silent for a moment.

Dan asked, 'What about that other stuff, the "change button" being on the inside. That didn't really click with me.'

'No pun intended,' Robbie remarked. Dan looked completely blank.

'The button. It didn't *click* with you. Get it?'

'Oh, very droll. Hilarious. You should be on the stage.' Dan was not amused.

'The meaning I took from it was that you have to want to change before change becomes possible. The "button on the inside" is just a way of expressing this,' Louise offered.

'A kind of readiness index,' Robbie said.

'Why don't we just ask Mr Cheung to explain it to us?' Dan suggested.

'Because, I suspect that he wants us to figure it out for ourselves. The questioning is part of the journey.' Once again, Robbie seemed momentarily lost in thought. In the process of answering Dan, the central idea seemed to have become clearer to him.

'Well, I signed up for fitness classes, not a course in fortune telling. Anyway, I don't need to reinvent myself.'

'And we do, Ed?' Robbie asked.

'That's not what I meant.'

'Well, that's how it came across.' An emerging tension between Robbie and Ed was evident.

'It's all a bit confusing,' Dan remarked. 'I mean, if you go into a shop to buy a suit, they don't try to sell you an umbrella. Why are we trying to interpret subtle philosophical messages from a fitness teacher who may never even have been to college?'

'Whoa. How do you know whether Mr Cheung has been to college or not? And anyway, what's that got to do with anything?' It was Louise's turn to show annoyance.

'Well, one thing's for sure,' Robbie observed. 'College or no college, he's certainly caught our attention.'

There was some additional small talk about work. As part of the ritual 'getting to know you' process, the group tentatively revealed some personal details and tried to make connections about people and places they knew. Tired, following the exercise and the conversation, they left for home.

Dan's Notebook 1

The next day, Dan was still puzzling about the core messages. During his scientific training he'd always been taught to write down the essence of a problem. In the drawer underneath his desk he found an unused spiral notebook. After a couple of scribbled attempts he captured the ideas put forward by Mr Cheung, adding some additional points for clarification.

Chapter 1

1.1 You are the Chief Executive (CEO) of your own life: If your life is happy you've made it so. If your life is unhappy, you're also responsible (by putting up with it). While 'bad things' might happen, you need to dictate how you respond to these. If you decide not to change, then someone or something else is essentially the CEO of your life. And, you've appointed them into the position!

1.2 The 'button for change' is on the inside: No one can force you to change. They can advise, criticise or cajole you – but only you can decide to change. You change either because the 'pain' (today's picture) is intolerable and pushes you to do something about it, or the 'prize' (tomorrow's picture) is emotionally compelling and pulls you forward. Without a clear pain or prize, personal change goes to the bottom of the in-tray. Nothing happens.

Okay, I sort of get it now, Dan thought. He carefully placed the notebook back in the drawer, locking it securely. It had tweaked his interest. He resolved to go to the self-help section of a bookstore he liked in the city, to bone-up on this stuff. Dan was like a pit-bull terrier with new ideas. Once he'd bitten one, he just wouldn't let go until he'd unscrambled the puzzle in his head.

Stretching the Muscles in Your Mind

The third training session was particularly tough – 25 minutes of stretching was followed by an exhausting dance routine. Mr Cheung, who could stretch like an elastic band, moved with cat-like flexibility.

A couple of people from the first night seemed to have dropped out, the normal desertion rate for 'New Year Resolution' classes. The exercises were so strenuous that, at one point, Dan had to take a break. He sat off to one side sipping a bottle of still water while the class continued. Louise felt like taking a breather, but hung in based on sheer will-power. Ed was absolutely knackered. He was up half the night with the new baby who had been crying non-stop. Teething time.

During the warm-down (gentle stretching exercises followed by deep breathing), Mr Cheung asked the group to reflect on what it was they really wanted. As they lay on the floor, he walked through the group, speaking quietly.

'We all desire things. Like car or holiday or new partner.' He smiled. 'Need decide what you really want. If you want something, how much you want it? Do you want enough to make happen, to change you life? You need understand big difference between pleasure and happiness. They not same thing. Sometimes opposite. Need to feed your spirit. Think about all these things and we talk again next week.'

Coffee Dock Counselling

In the juice bar, Robbie placed the order. After the rigors of the class, everyone opted for a caffeine hit, by-passing the healthier options. He brought the drinks across to the round table where they normally sat. Their routine had quickly become established.

'Well, what did you make of tonight's lesson?' Louise asked.

'Actually, I found it quite tough. I had to take a break to catch my breath.'

'I don't mean the class itself, Dan,' Louise said kindly. 'What did you make of the bit at the end, the big question: "*What do you really want?*"'

'It seems deceptively simple, but it's not,' Robbie suggested. Socrates said: "The unexamined life is not worth living".'

'"Socrates said." Wow, we're really into the heavy hitters now.'

'Ed, I don't know why everything I say seems to irk you. I assure you it's not deliberate. But your cynicism is pissing me off.'

'I'm pissing *you* off? Every week you come here, flaunting your superiority. You look down on the rest of us.'

'Hey guys. Stop the lights. Can you play this matador game somewhere else? I have to put up with enough crap during the day without volunteering for it at night.' Louise was bluntly assertive. 'Now if we are over the theatrics can we get back to the question, "what is it that you really want?"'

'I can't just re-focus like that. If I come across as acting superior, believe me it's a great act.' Robbie looked agitated. He continued, 'But, maybe there's something else going on here.'

'Yeah? Like what?'

'Ed, no doubt you will think this is more waffle but here goes anyway. There's a concept in psychotherapy called projection.'

'Enlighten me.'

'The idea is that feelings you have inside yourself, sometimes unconscious feelings that you may not be fully aware of, get "projected" onto someone else. Essentially, you see in others things that you are feeling inside yourself.'

'Oh, I can see where this is going. It's not that you act in a superior way, it's me all the time. I feel inferior and somehow you get the blame for this.'

'You project your own feelings onto someone else. That's precisely it.' As far as Robbie was concerned Ed needed to look in the mirror – rather than scapegoat everyone else for his feelings.

'I don't buy all that psycho-babble,' Ed stated, somewhat unconvincingly. He seemed a bit rattled.

Dan, who had not really been following the conversation, interrupted the moment. 'I've been thinking about this "what do you really want" question and it's quite confusing. I mean, I know what I *have* and I sort of know what I *don't want*. But, apart from a few material things, it's difficult to say what I *really* want.'

'Why is it difficult?' Louise asked, glad to move the focus away from Robbie and Ed.

'I'm not sure.' He hesitated. 'Maybe because I've never really thought about it. My life has been a series of next steps. College, getting married, promotion. I don't think that anything was ever planned, not in any formal sense.'

'I can relate to that,' Robbie said. 'It's not that

you don't do *any* planning, but ... the planning is around individual achievements, not based on an end goal.'

'That's exactly my point,' Dan nodded vigorously.

'What is it that you want, Ed?' Louise was hoping to heal the earlier rift by pulling Ed back into the conversation.

'Right now I just want to drink this coffee and head for the hills.' Ed would not play the game.

'Can I ask you a personal question?' Robbie looked directly at Ed.

'You can ask, but I'm not necessarily going to answer it.'

'Why did you take up the 'Dance-Boxing' classes?'

'I told you the first night. I'm busy at work. It takes up 80 per cent of my focus. No one watches the clock. Then there's a lot going on at home. That takes up the other 80 per cent. I need down time to let some of the air out of the balloon.'

'And has it worked out?' Dan asked a rare question.

'Well, it was okay, up to tonight anyway. Look, maybe I'm just overtired. Talk to you.' Ed pushed back his chair, stood up and left.

'Jesus, his spring is tight,' Dan remarked when Ed was gone.

'Running the ruler over your life is tough for all of us. Maybe he just needs a bit of space.' Given the earlier conversation, Robbie's words were surprisingly empathetic.

'Maybe we all need some chill time,' Louise agreed.

'I know what I need,' Dan said. 'To buy a bottle of anti-rheumatism spray. I will be stiff as a poker in the morning.'

'Now, now, don't be boasting,' Robbie teased. It took Dan a moment to get the joke.

'No, no. You picked me up *completely* wrong,' he protested.

'Relax, Dan. You're one of the good guys.' Louise was laughing openly.

Outside it was pitch dark. Cloud cover had blocked any potential moonlight. Louise was still smiling as she packed her gym gear into the boot of the car and headed home.

Dan's Notebook 2

The following morning, Dan retrieved the notebook. He began to scribble a couple of rough ideas, then tore out the page and carefully re-wrote the notes. Similar to the first week, he added some of his own thoughts, fleshing out the skeleton provided by Mr Cheung.

Chapter 2

2.1 What is it you want? What would a 'better tomorrow' look like? What would the key elements be? Don't be constrained by thinking about what exists today; tomorrow could be radically different. Dare to dream about a better space. Think big thoughts.

2.2 How much do you want it? Personal change is possible – if you want it badly enough to do something about it, i.e. if the gain outweighs the pain. Do you want it enough to take on the challenge of changing your life? Ask yourself: What would I like to change about myself or my life?

2.3 Make your desires 'graphic': Make the tomorrow picture easier to see by 'chunking' it into components, making each piece as graphic as possible.

- **Wealth/financial status**
- **Family**
- **Career success**
- **Health**
- **Social contribution**
- **Leisure time**

2.4 Pleasure vs happiness: One is a short-term feeling of elation; the other is a slower burn, but provides deeper contentment. Chasing pleasure is not the route to happiness – they are often opposites. Happiness is more often a 'by-product' – you encounter it when doing something else which is important or worthwhile. It is like a shadow. If you chase after it directly – it seems to move away.

23

I am beginning to understand the basic points, Dan thought. *None of this is rocket science. But, it's hard to find the time to follow through on this stuff.*

He walked back over to address the bench chemistry problem he'd been working on for several weeks. Tiny black specks had been occurring in batches of pharmaceutical product – and no one could pinpoint the source of the contaminant. Somehow, it seemed simpler to resolve. At least he knew that there was an answer, somewhere, waiting to be discovered.

Back At the Ranch

Ed was upset after the run-in with Robbie. Not about the argument per se (he was well used to dealing with conflict in his job), but somehow the incident had touched a raw nerve. The pushback from Robbie – that he should take a look in the mirror before striking out – hit home. Yet, while he felt an unease, he wasn't sure what to do about it.

This fitness group was quirky. He definitely didn't like Robbie who seemed to have elected himself as the unofficial chairperson of the group. During one of the off-line discussions, it emerged that Dan had a PhD in some obscure branch of science. As far as Ed was concerned, Dan might be smart, in a bookish way, but he seemed a complete gobshite otherwise. He hadn't a titter of wit. Then there was Louise. Now she was interesting. Smart, good-looking, single, maybe even a bit vulnerable …

The physical stuff was first-class. Ed was already in good shape but the classes were really toning him up. Mr Cheung was incredible. It was almost worth putting up with the corny philosophy to get access to the exercise programme. Almost.

While the dynamics were weird, Ed resolved to keep going along for the moment. *Maybe I'll take a back seat for a couple of sessions, take the heat down a notch or two.* He was interrupted by a high-pitched wail. The 'surprise' child needed to be fed and it was his shift.

6:20 pm: Ready, Steady . . .

The house was a mess. Louise had resolved to blitz it at the weekend but somehow hadn't gotten around to doing anything. At work she was part of a small project team. They were in an intense bidding phase for a major new bio-technology facility. Everyone was putting in long hours. After a long week, she'd spent most of Sunday with her mother on the receiving end of the 'Five Sorrowful Mysteries'.

I know you've lost your husband, but … I've lost my dad. He was my buddy, my teacher, the person in the world

25

who loved me most. All of these thoughts were left unsaid but deeply felt. Louise was becoming increasingly frustrated with her mother's 'grieving widow' role. It offered a single negative bucket into which all her miseries seemed to be dumped. *It wasn't always like this,* Louise reflected. But somehow she felt powerless to change the current situation.

Even as these thoughts washed over her, Louise felt guilty. What was the solution here? That her mother would order *The Power of Positive Thinking* from Amazon.com and become an immediate convert? Or was she secretly hoping her mother would die and 'unburden her'? This idea struck Louise as being so utterly selfish, she instantly pushed it out of her mind – like a sour taste that had to be spat out.

It all seemed pretty far removed from Mr Cheung's idea of the 'button for change being on the inside'. She felt manipulated, caught between the opposing pillars of outward caring and secret resentment. Somewhat down, Louise could barely raise the energy to pack her training bag and face the drive across the East Link bridge to Executive Fitness.

What's Blocking What You Want?

The beginning of the fourth exercise class was very strange. Mr Cheung put on a dance beat CD and the group was instructed to leap frog in a continuous circle, as fast as possible. It seemed childish and the result was disastrous. They eventually fell into disarray on the floor, laughing openly.

In the next exercise they had to make their way as quickly as possible through a tunnel of legs, with all the risqué fun which that entailed. It was juvenile and extremely funny. Class time seemed to buzz along at twice the normal speed. By the end of the session, Louise was exhausted but elated. Even Dan, normally somewhat dour, was upbeat.

'I haven't laughed so much in years,' he said.

'That was better than sex,' Ed offered.

'I'll take your word for that,' Robbie quipped, and everyone laughed. They sat around the wall, leaning back to support tired muscles.

Mr Cheung walked to the centre of the room and turned to face the group. 'You enjoy tonight session?' Everyone nodded.

'What usually stop you having fun?'

'My wife,' Ed said, which brought a further round of laughter. Mr Cheung smiled and waited until the humour subsided.

'To understand question, you need know yourself very well. In China we say three things make you happy. Number 1: Something to do. Be busy. Number 2: Someone to love. You understand? Number 3: Something to look forward to. Better future.'

He waited for a moment before continuing. 'Next week I want you focus on what stop you from laughing. Did you laugh more one time, when younger? Why you change? You understand what make you laugh, you understand who you are. Also consider "three things you need to be happy". This very strong message. Thank you for making *me* happy tonight. Make me forget own problems.'

Mr Cheung left the room, smiling openly.

Another Night at the Round Table

In the coffee dock, Louise ordered a latté for a change (*my system couldn't hack a power drink at this hour of the night*), while Dan and Ed had regular coffee. Robbie was married to juice. By the time they'd ordered, the earlier mood had dampened down. Dan was tired and seemed cranky.

'Look, I don't want to come across as a fuddy duddy. But you can't just go around the place laughing like a two-year-old. You'd get locked up.'

'I sort of agree. We all like a bit of craic, but it's Pollyannaish to think that you can just laugh your way through real issues,' Louise reflected.

'Maybe we're taking it too literally. The message was subtle.'

'And Robbie, you're going to single-handedly interpret this complex message and make it simple for us,' said Ed.

'Ed, why don't you *add* to the conversation instead of always subtracting.'

'I'm interested in what you have to say, Robbie. I may not agree with it, but I won't know that until I hear it. Go ahead.'

The rebuke from Louise was stinging and Ed's face flushed. He pushed his chair back from the table and sat off to one side.

'Hey Robbie. The pressure is on now. This analysis better be good!' Louise teased.

'Okay. Look, I don't think that Mr Cheung meant for us to sign up for a season ticket to the Comedy Lounge. But ... if you can figure out what's *stopping* you from being happy, maybe there is a way to remove the "roadblock".'

'I'm not disagreeing,' Dan said. 'But it's kind of obvious. Is this a big insight or am I missing something?'

'Well, it might be simple but it's not simplistic: 2 + 2 = 4. While the maths are simple, they are also correct. Look, I don't know any more about this stuff than anyone else, but I can relate to the sentiment. That's all I'm saying.'

'And that is because ...?' Louise asked.

'Eh ... this is getting a bit personal.'

'Don't reveal anything you're not comfortable with. No forced confessions.'

'Thanks, Louise, I understand that. It's just knowing where to begin. Okay, well first off, I'm gay. You probably knew that, or guessed it, already.'

Louise and Ed simply nodded while Dan exclaimed, 'You're *gay*?'

'Yeah, it's right up there on the psychotic list beside serial killer.'

'Sorry Robbie, that came out wrong. It's just, I'd really no idea.'

'Okay, Dan. It's not a problem.'

'Go on with the issue. Something about the "stopping you from laughing" idea made sense,' Louise reminded Robbie about the point he was making.

'Well, it's stupid, particularly at my age, but

I've never officially told my family. I know that they know. And they've met Alan, my partner, whom I introduced as a friend. But it's still sort of *undiscussable*.'

'Why haven't you told them?' The question from Ed was direct but the tone was softer, not challenging.

Robbie took a deep breath and seemed to settle himself. 'I'm not 100 per cent sure. My father is a bit of a man's man. He played hurling at county level with Clare and he's always been conservative.'

'And you sense that he would be uncomfortable with you being gay – because he would see that as effeminate?' Louise held eye contact, waiting for the reply.

'Yeah, sort of. And ... maybe something else.'

'Just take it to where you want,' Louise repeated her earlier caution.

'I love my dad and my mother. I've no wish, absolutely zero, to hurt them in any way. I owe them both so much. But at some level I feel that I'm living a lie. It seems insincere. No, not insincere – false.'

It was said in such a heartfelt way that the group were not quite sure how to respond.

'That's what's stopping me from laughing. I can't really be happy until I resolve this and I'm not sure what to do about it.'

'How old is your dad?' Dan asked.

'He's 66', Louise answered. 'We discussed it at an earlier session.'

'Oh, that's right, I remember now. No real joy there then.'

'That's a bit cryptic. No real joy about what?' Louise asked.

'Look, I get it. At that age he's likely to be around for another while. If he was 75, or 80, the problem would take care of itself sooner rather than later, isn't that it Dan?' Robbie was smiling.

'I know it's crass, but I've had the same thought myself. No, he's as healthy as a farmer's baby.'

Louise looked thoughtful, somewhat hesitant even. 'This is not a well formed question, but aren't you giving your parents a lot of power?'

'In what sense?'

'You're making the point that your parents, well your dad in particular, may not accept that you're gay.' Robbie nodded.

'But you're not comfortable with the status quo. You feel inauthentic, sort of living a lie, to use your own phrase.'

'You were certainly listening.'

'Robbie, I'm going to take a risk here ...'

'Hmmm. Okay. Go for it Louise. I promise not to ignite!'

'It seems to me that you have a couple of choices. You can tell your mother and father and see what happens or don't tell them and continue as is.'

'That's about it. Eh ... are you holding something back?'

'Well, if you really buy into the CEO of your own life idea, which I think you do, you wouldn't allow your parents to control your happiness. Trust me, I'm pretty expert on this particular question. So, my guess is that there's something else? Let me spin the question a different way. Suppose you did tell them, what's the worst that could happen?'

'I don't know. They'd be shocked. Maybe angry. Disappointed. They might need time to work it through ...'

'None of that seems too terrible.' Louise was challenging the logic.

'Now that I actually say it, it doesn't.'

'So what's holding you back from telling them?'

'I'm not ... sure,' Robbie seemed less certain now.

Dan interjected, 'When I was a kid I went to the zoo with my dad and ended up getting lost. I'll never forget how scared I was. It was terrifying.'

'And your point is?' Ed remarked.

'It's obvious. Being separated from your parents is scary.'

'Dan, that was when you were a child.' Louise seemed a bit confused about where the conversation was going.

'Yeah, I know. But maybe it doesn't change all that much.'

The group was silent for a couple of moments.

'What do you think you will do, Robbie?' Louise asked.

'I'm not really sure, not yet anyway. But I need to address this particular issue. It's as if a fog has shifted.'

'This *particular* issue ... ?' she quizzed.

'Don't even go there. I've taken up enough couch time for one evening. Next week I'm in listening mode. The big ear. All the way.'

'Robbie, you've been hugely helpful to this group. No worries. You were due a bit of attention', Louise was smiling encouragement.

'I agree. And I'd absolutely no idea you were *gay*,' Dan said.

'Oh for God's sake. This is too hard, let's call it a day.' Louise stood up to leave, visibly annoyed.

Dan touched Robbie's shoulder in a gesture of support, a silent 'no offence meant'.

Sitting off to one side, Ed seemed uncomfortable with the conversation. The 'opening up' at the session had been intense. *What if you tried all this stuff and nothing worked? What then?* While he found himself more and more attracted to Louise, where this group stuff was going was anyone's guess. Perhaps it was time to talk to Louise on her own.

'Hey, what about the remark right at the end of the class. "You make me forget own problems".' Dan tried to imitate Mr Cheung's accent.

'Who knows?' Robbie said. 'Maybe we should pick up on that some other time. It's not that we're short of our own agendas to work through.'

Everyone nodded. It was time to cut the cord for another night.

Dan's Notebook 3

If routine was a subject, Dan was a definite 'A' student. First thing on Wednesday morning, he found the key, opened the drawer in his desk and slid out the spiral notebook. Pushed for time, he quickly scribbled down the central points that Mr Cheung had raised, adding a couple of thoughts of his own.

Chapter 3

3.1 Stopping you laughing: What is it that stops you laughing? What holds you back? Is it something, i.e. the fear of looking foolish, or someone, i.e. a particular person? If you seemed happier at one point in your life, what changed? Understanding this is a clue to what you really enjoy.

3.2 Philosophy of happiness: Do you have something to do, someone to love and something to look forward to? What areas of your life mean the most to you? What issues need most attention? While there are always 'lots of things' to change – one or two of these could make a real breakthrough for you. What are they?

The discipline of capturing the ideas was comforting to Dan. It gave them an 'order'. Right now there was a lot on at work. Thinking through the individual issues raised would have to wait until another time. He closed the notebook and carefully placed it back in its allotted space, promising himself that he'd get to it later. Definitely.

What Do You Stand For?

By the fifth class, the attendance had dropped right off. It was now down to the core group: Robbie, Dan, Louise and Ed. They acknowledged each other at the beginning of the class.

The fifth exercise session was so tough, it bordered on cruelty. Even the preliminary warm-up routine was torturous. Muscles stretched to the limit, and then some. The group was held in taut positions for what seemed an eternity. 'Keep stretching those leg muscles, long time. You tired tonight.'

Mr Cheung, normally positive and warm, seemed somehow distant. He pushed the group through each exercise, minus the good humoured cajoling which they'd come to expect. At the end of what seemed like the longest exercise class, he addressed the group directly.

'It very important to know what you stand for. You know why?' Tired and somewhat gloomy, no one ventured a guess.

'Because you don't know what you stand for, you no have compass. You don't stand for something, you fall for anything. You need reflect on this. Second, surrender to fact that life not fair. Expect fairness, you all time disappointed. Let me give example. Playing poker, some people get bad cards. But, in life, you not stuck with cards given. Possible to change them. Not stuck with – this difficult word – legacy from family.'

Without saying goodnight or goodbye, he abruptly left the room.

In the Coffee Dock: Mr Cheung's Ideas on Trial

'The question posed by Mr Cheung, "what do you stand for?" Is that similar to your personal values? Like I don't steal or drink and drive.'

'Dan, I'm not sure that there are any absolutes here. We're all muddling through this stuff.' Robbie always addressed Dan in a friendly tone.

'What's your take on it, Robbie?' Louise asked.

'It *could* be something to do with personal beliefs. But for me it was more around the idea of having a central goal. A couple of years ago I read about a concept called psycho-cybernetics. Bear with me Ed, this one is worth a spin.'

'I hadn't opened my mouth.'

'The basic idea is that if you have a clearly stated purpose, you automatically begin to move towards it without even realising that you are doing so.'

'That fits with my understanding of cybernetics. It's a Greek word meaning goal-striving. For example, the mechanisms used in guided missiles are cybernetic.' Dan was pleased to be able to demonstrate his scientific knowledge.

Robbie continued. 'How do you remember all that stuff? Anyway, the "what do you stand for" idea mentioned tonight seemed quite similar.'

'And how do you figure it out? I mean, exactly what you stand for?' Dan asked.

'This course doesn't come with a Ladybird guide.' Ed's comment was caustic.

'Did you specifically learn how to be offensive or does it just come naturally?' Robbie felt the need to defend Dan. In his view, Ed had become an enormous 'pain in the arse', a totally negative influence on the group. He was closed to the ideas being discussed. Why did he bother coming to the classes?

'Maybe you enjoy playing the "bold boy" role. Is that it, Ed? Lots of practise. Hard to change the habits of a lifetime.'

Ed's face flushed red with anger. 'You know

fuck all about me. You've no shortage of your own issues to work through without playing the amateur psychologist on me.'

'Lads, give it a rest. This game is becoming tiresome and I think I finally know why. It's easier to go into the caveman routine than wrestling with the stuff that these sessions are throwing up. We're not here to win a debating contest.'

On a roll now, Robbie would not allow himself to be deflected. He ignored Louise's comment and continued. 'Come on Ed, let's drill into it. What's really eating you? You sneer at the process, like those two old guys in the Muppets – shouting down narky comments about what's happening on the stage. Why?'

'I signed up for exercise classes. I'm trying to keep fit, not sane.'

'It's more than just Ed,' Louise intervened. 'This is getting close to the bone for all of us. The process is challenging who we are and how we live.'

'Wow! It's not just one. I've discovered a whole nest of psychoanalysts or psychiatrists – whatever you think you are. Well here's a bit of *new* news. Some of us are happy in our own skin. Some of us have a life, a real job *and* a family.' He stared at Louise and Robbie. 'If the rest of you need this new-age crap to deal with your hang-ups, that's okay by me. But the recipe doesn't apply to everyone. And if you think I'm avoiding anything, you're right. I *will* be avoiding this dipstick group analysis. Sayonara!' Ed stood up and walked away abruptly.

After he left, the mood in the group was sombre. 'Maybe it did seem like an attack.' Louise was remorseful, feeling that they'd pushed Ed over the edge.

'Don't sweat it, he had it coming. Whatever the opposite of charisma is, Ed has loads of it.' Robbie was unsympathetic.

'Or maybe we're veering off track,' Dan offered.

'Oh! How so?'

'One of the early ideas was that "the change button is on the inside". Maybe we are trying to change Ed from the outside. I don't think he's ready for it.'

Robbie looked stunned.

'I don't mean to be patronising, Dan, but that's bang on.' He took a moment to reflect on his own role in the dialogue with Ed.

'It's a useful reminder to all of us,' Louise concurred.

'Scientific types have their uses, you know.' Dan was pleased, basking in the rare compliment.

'I know this is a struggle, but I think that some good will come out of it,' Louise mused.

'Yeah, if we ever go to a salsa night that degenerates into a kickboxing session we will be well primed on both fronts.' Robbie put on a look of mock sincerity and they laughed.

'A tiny bit of cynicism creeping in Robbie?' Louise teased.

'Maybe just a tad.'

As they were walking out to the car-park, Louise disclosed to the group that she was wrestling with a personal dilemma and wanted some airtime to discuss it at their next session.

'Want to give us a sneak preview?' Robbie asked.

'No, it'll hold.'

Dan's Notebook 4

By now Dan had his 'notebook routine' down pat. He normally arrived at work before 8.00 am – well ahead of the posse. It beat the traffic and gave him time to collect his thoughts. Each Wednesday morning he captured the notes from the Dance-Boxing classes. He flipped over to a blank page.

Chapter 4

4.1 What do you stand for? Is there one central purpose in your life – one 'big idea'? Maybe there's more than one. What are these key concepts which you firmly believe in? What is it that you are here to do, your personal mission? How do you want to be remembered? How will you make a difference?

4.2 Where did it originate? Did your 'big idea' come from your family/upbringing? Did it develop because of a significant emotional experience? What is the drive/the payoff? How will life be better for you if you achieve this purpose?

4.3 Life is not fair: Not everyone is born with equal gifts. Some have great physical assets; others don't. Some people have terrific parents and supportive families; others don't. Sometimes terrible things happen – seemingly at random – which could not in any sense be described as fair. You need to 'surrender' to the idea that life is not fair, rather than keep railing against it. There is no sense that the route forward will always be linear; you may go backwards. But even when it is unfair, you remain the Chief Executive of your own life. You own your response to whatever happens.

These questions don't have any easy answers. Just then the phone rang and he was transported back into his real world. Allowing himself to be distracted was easy but Dan knew he'd have to find a better way to engage with this stuff. Knowing that the material was there and he was not systematically working through it was starting to weigh down on him.

The Latin Night

When it came to dancing, Mr Cheung could not be described as a 'natural'. While he was unbelievably flexible and fit, his rhythm was less than pronounced. During the sixth class, they played a succession of Latin beats, sambas, cha-cha's and rumbas. As the group moved with the beat, the music was infectious. Dan was so uncoordinated it was painfully funny. Even Mr Cheung, normally a little straight, was laughing openly.

It was amazing. In a few short weeks the group had taken their fitness to a new level. They now trained continuously, without stopping for a break every ten minutes which had characterised the earlier classes. At the end of a particularly high-spirited class, they completed the warm-down exercises and sat against the walls, waiting for Mr Cheung to begin.

After several minutes of silence, Ed asked, 'What's the name of this particular game? Is it the "silent school of counselling"?'

He smiled at his own punch line and looked at the others to garner support. No one responded. Their body language told Ed this would be a solo run.

After another couple of silent minutes and almost unbearable tension, Dan intervened. 'I'm getting a bit edgy here. There may well be some purpose to what we are doing but it's not obvious. I don't like being part of something I don't understand.'

Mr Cheung held eye contact with Dan for a moment but said nothing. Everyone shifted nervously in position, moving around to try to get more comfortable. Ed stood up.

'I don't do mystery tours. Adios Amigos.' He turned and started to walk towards the exit.

'Ed, why you wish to leave?' Mr Cheung asked the question gently.

'I'm not a boy and I'm not playing schoolboy games.'

'Why you think it a game?'

'It's not natural. Sitting around waiting for you to say something and then you give us the silent treatment.'

'What is your ... *expectation*?'

45

'I ... I thought we'd do the usual. You'd come up with some, eh, new philosophy or insight and the class would finish. Like normal.'

Mr Cheung nodded, signalling that he understood the point. 'Please rejoin us. Trust me.'

Ed sat back down, somewhat reluctantly. Mr Cheung now addressed the full group.

'Each class, I have been leader. I lead exercise, then discussion. You expect me in charge. This okay in class. Not okay in life. You must be leader. You decide what you want. When someone else become leader, this give comfort. But it no good. Lead own life, much better. Take control of own life, this my personal struggle. Not trying to change is failure.'

The depth of emotion in his voice could not be mistaken. Mr Cheung seemed visibly upset, almost teary. He stood up, nodded to the group, and quietly left the room.

Solving the Problems of the World: At the Bar

'Jesus, that was weird. The silence only lasted a couple of minutes but it was disturbing.' Louise had ordered the coffees and taken up the running.

'To be honest, I found it okay. I knew that it was being done to make *some* point and we'd eventually get to it. I was sort of enjoying the *calmness*.' Robbie was smiling.

'I'm with Louise,' Dan said. 'I like Mr Cheung and the fitness stuff but some of the philosophy and the ways used to communicate it are just too obscure.'

Ed added, 'Whatever about the method, the fundamental message is flawed. Look at my case. The job is 24/7. Manufacturing is full of sharks. It's eat or be eaten. You have to stay awake. After work, the kids and herself are full-on. Maybe the "lead yourself" message works well for unmarried civil servants, but it doesn't apply to me.'

'Do you feel trapped?' Robbie asked.

'No, I don't feel trapped,' Ed said defensively.

'I took on the job and I can leave when I want. The kids are just at an awkward age, that's all. Another couple of years and I won't have to worry about them. And, I get to go home most nights,' he added grinning, trying to stave off the inquiry.

'So, maybe you are already *leading* in your life. You have the purpose figured, and you are getting there.' Robbie's tone was tinged with sarcasm.

'Yeah, maybe I am.'

'You seem angry a lot of the time,' Dan observed with his trademark directness.

'I'm just pissed off with these afterburn, meditation sessions.'

'Ed, I know we asked you before, but why do you continue to come here?' Louise looked at him directly.

'I'm ... not sure. Look, I don't want to be pouring cold water on this stuff. You guys seem to be enjoying it and getting something out of it. I'm not sure it's for me, that's all.'

'The questions seem pretty universal. "Who am I? What do I want to do with my life? What's blocking me from doing this?" They'd apply to most people – unless you were in some awful predicament – in jail or a slave or something.' Robbie would not give up the point easily.

'We are all vulnerable here, Ed; you don't have a monopoly on feeling insecure.' Ed did not respond to Louise's prompt and stayed silent.

'Will you continue to come to the classes?' Dan asked.

'Probably. I'd miss all this fun if I left.'

'Well, whatever you decide is good with me. I'm sure it's good with all of us.' Louise seemed to feel some responsibility for keeping Ed within the group.

'Okay Louise, it's over to you now. Last week you promised to reveal the big "mystery". This is *dilemma discussion night*.' Robbie wanted to switch gears and move the conversation along.

'I think I need another caffeine hit for this

one.' As the second coffee was being prepared, Louise told her story. She tried to steer a line between truthfulness and berating her mother, which seemed disrespectful. A couple of minutes later she finished the monologue with a playful 'and ... the answer is?'

'It's not an easy one,' Robbie said, sympathetically.

'A guy in work had a very similar problem with his father, almost identical in fact.'

'Go on, Dan. Tell us how this fits with Louise's dilemma.' Robbie was always amused by Dan's circuitous communication style.

'Well, it doesn't really. Just demonstrates that the issue is quite common.'

'Yeah! Hands up whoever had a mother or father,' Ed said scathingly.

'I won't lower myself to respond to that.' Dan, normally tolerant of Ed, was not amused.

'Was it something Mr Cheung said that pushed you into thinking about your relationship with your mum?' Robbie asked, ignoring Ed's provocation.

'Very much so. I mentioned before that "the CEO for your own life" idea really hit home. Normally at work I'm reasonably confident. Engineering and construction are male-dominated industries. Shrinking violets tend not to last too long. But, when it comes to my mother, any normal assertiveness seems to be diluted by guilt.'

'Problem solving is not always either-or,' Dan suggested.

'I'm listening, Dan. Just not sure I'm with you.' Louise was smiling.

'You present the story about your mother in an either-or configuration. Either you look after her needs, and virtually abandon your own, or you ignore your mother completely and selfishly pursue your agenda.'

'I'm still not following.'

'It's sometimes possible to come to a negotiated settlement. Oh God, I'm not explaining this very well.' Dan looked momentarily confused, then continued. 'Okay, suppose a husband likes to play golf and his wife resents the time away from the family.'

'Okay.'

'Well, he could give up playing golf altogether or he could just ignore his wife and continue playing.'

'In either case, one party would feel hard done by,' Robbie clarified.

'Exactly. But rather than taking an either-or approach, they could come to a negotiated settlement. Like playing golf once a week, say on Saturdays.'

'I think I'm beginning to see the point. Rather than feeling burdened by looking after my mother all the time, I could set some sort of boundary around this?'

'When you suit yourself, you end up suiting everyone.'

'That's clever Dan. Simple, but clever. It has a sort of "horse sense".'

'Well, it's something for you to think about.'

'Hey Dan, you are even starting to sound like Mr Cheung now,' Robbie teased.

'I will think about it.' Louise seemed genuinely pleased. 'Thanks for your time, all of you. I hope I can reciprocate.'

'You already have.' The remark from Ed was a little puzzling and the group did not quite know how to respond. Moments later they called it a night and headed home.

Dan's Notebook 5

Due to an early meeting, Dan did not have time the following morning to update his notes. During a quiet moment, just after lunch, he scanned through the first couple of entries in his notebook before adding the following:

Chapter 5

5.1 Being in control: *Are you taking control of your own life? Are you making-it-happen or saying 'what happened'? Are you secretly taking comfort in allowing someone else to lead your life or using this as an 'escape clause' for regrets or disappointments? The good news is you can be in control. The bad news is once you accept this, you can't outsource the blame.*

5.2 Stepping up to the line: *If you take on a leadership responsibility, and subsequently fail, there will be no one to blame. But, what is the opposite? Do you want to spend your life following someone else's agenda? You own the responsibility to make your own life a success (however you define this). It can be different (if you want it to be). What stops most people is the fear of failure – when the only real failure is not trying.*

It was one thing to 'capture' the notes but quite another to make sense of them (or come up with exact answers to the questions posed). Some of the questions were simple enough; others seemed abstract and unsettling. He checked his watch. The next meeting was in five minutes so that put an end to Dan's philosophical musings for the day. He wondered what, if anything, he could do with the notebook. A plan was starting to form in his mind.

Sometimes the 'Wave' is Bigger than the Swimmer

Ed was in a quandary. Despite his outward show of resistance, the questions posed by Mr Cheung and the group were beginning to unsettle him. At work, he normally had a reasonable sense of humour and was able to 'acquit himself' well in social situations. Yet, the dynamic of the Dance-Boxing group was somehow different. He'd gotten off to a bad start which had continued to go downhill. Rapidly.

The middle child in a family of five, Ed still felt strong competition with his siblings. They were a stereotypically successful bunch. His eldest brother was a barrister who'd made huge money working the tribunals circuit. Two other brothers ran a successful construction company, riding high on the house building frenzy. His sister was a well-known graphic artist. All of them had gone to university or art college. Ed had rebelled and joined his current employer as a junior. Over the years he'd clawed his way up the 'slippery corporate pole' as he referred to it. Being head of purchasing was de facto recognition of his deep understanding of the business. His ability to shave suppliers' prices, honed over many years of negotiations, was legendary. He was well-off, but not wealthy. *It's difficult for wage slaves to ever own the boat,* was Ed's favourite saying. All the new kids coming into the business had been to university. Some of them had more degrees than a thermometer and it was hard not to feel threatened by them.

Ed had seriously thought about going back to study (a couple of colleges, recognising the value of his work experience, would have gladly accepted him) but the time dilemma was always acute. Tough job, three young kids plus studying – it didn't compute. A core goal for Ed was to build financial security, a nest egg that would make life easier for his children than it had been for him. *There's only one thing worse than being old. It's being old and poor.* A strong memory was visiting an older aunt who'd ended her days in St. Mary's Hospital in the Phoenix Park. *I don't want to end up living in some 'granny farm', being fed with a plastic spoon.* He didn't feel it was appropriate to discuss his goals or his financial concerns with people whom he barely knew. *Life coaching from Dan? Gimme a break!* he thought.

More recently Ed noticed that he'd begun to resent other people's lifestyles. Robbie, in particular, seemed to be 'rolling in it' – turning up each week wearing more labels than Naomi Campbell. Louise had no kids which allowed her to punch in long hours and do what she liked after work. Dan's kids had left the nest and working in the sleepy pharmaceutical industry probably allowed him tons of time off. As far as Ed was concerned, they all had time to think about this personal change stuff. He didn't.

However, Louise was really cute. *If I could just get her back on track ...* He decided to give it one more spin and see what happened. There was nothing to lose at this stage.

You've Got Mail

Louise's phone was making that annoying 'beep' sound. She opened the message minder. One unread. A further click revealed the following:

```
Hi Louise. Know dat I've been bit
of a prat in grp but hve decided
2 face up 2 it. Lt goin on at the
mo which I hvnt been fully able 2
```

discuss. Keen 2 get more feedback
from u. Wud luv 2 meet separately
4 a beer or coffee. Whatever. Do
me this favour? Ed.

She read the message a couple of times. Was this on the level, a genuine call for support or a thinly veiled pass? It was impossible to judge from the tone. Tempted to reply, she held off. It needed more thought. As she was thinking about how to respond, her mother called with a shopping list of chores – packaged in the *It's difficult to cope on your own* speech. Louise could feel the tension mounting as her mother ranted on. She managed to reassure her mam that the individual jobs would be completed sometime before global warming flooded the earth. It was not the right time to broach the broader subject, until she had put it together in her mind. After the call from her mother, Louise read the text message again, still confused about the intent.

Executive Fitness Club: Achieving Balance

Mr Cheung stated clearly at the front-end of the class that he was going to focus on balance. He then introduced a number of exercises which the group performed, trying to mirror his free-flowing movements.

The first couple of moves were relatively easy, but became progressively more difficult. Louise was standing directly behind Robbie and could see dark patches of perspiration appear on his Nike top. As usual Ed was well ahead of the class. He had great natural ability. While the balance exercises seemed simple, they were surprisingly tiring. A couple of weeks earlier Louise had gone to a performance of the Chinese State Circus; she now better understood the level of difficulty of the routines they'd performed.

At the end of the class, as had become customary, Mr Cheung led the discussion.

'We coming close to end of programme. I think you ready for one final big idea. I call this "How to get there". You already spend time asking "Who am I" to help you understand yourself and what you need to do to become leader in own life. The question "What do I want?" help you look at better tomorrow. It help lots if picture of tomorrow very clear. Final question, "How will I get there?" Cannot become someone different by remaining what you are. Person on top of mountain not fall there.'

Normally Dan was constrained during Mr Cheung's address and held off until the group debriefing to clear up any misunderstanding, but he blurted out, 'When you say, "How will I get

57

there", what *exactly* are you proposing?'

Mr Cheung regarded Dan for a moment, his look something between perplexity and fatherly amusement.

'You begin practical steps to put life on right road. Road that leads towards tomorrow.'

Dan looked at him blankly.

'You think about it. We talk again next week. If necessary.'

Latté Debriefing Session

To change the scenery, Robbie suggested going to a pub for the weekly debriefing exercise. Everyone agreed and they adjourned to O'Brien's. The small lounge at the back of the pub was normally quiet on Tuesday nights – ideal for their purposes. After they'd ordered drinks, Dan, who seemed a bit agitated, asked, 'What did you make of that answer? It still isn't clear to me what he meant.'

'Dan, you should know the story by now. You have to come up with your own interpretation.' Robbie's tone was kindly.

'Yeah! It's not painting-by-numbers,' Ed added.

'But if it's not clear, how can you do anything about it?' Dan countered.

'On one level I agree with you, Dan', Louise

offered. 'It does need to be clear. But it's up to each of us to work through the concepts. *That's* where the clarity comes from. Bouncing ideas around in the group has helped to clarify some of this stuff for me. You have to put your own spin on it.'

'That could be absolutely right. Or the whole thing could be a complete spoof. A bucket of smoke,' Ed offered. Louise had not replied to the text message. As far as Ed was concerned that was a straightforward rejection – so there really was no need to keep up any pretence.

'And, because you're so smart, your in-built bullshit detector has the power to cut through the charade.' Louise was sick of Ed's sniping.

'I don't know about bullshit detection in general, but I can smell the "wannabe" aspirations in this group.' Ed was in cynical overdrive.

'And how about yourself? What are you going to change? Or maybe it's impossible to improve on perfection.' Louise held her ground.

'I think you might be having this conversation with the wrong person. Perhaps you should take up your issues with your moany mother.'

Louise visibly paled. 'That's a cheap shot. It's actually below you, Ed. Is this something to do with the text message?'

'What text message?' Dan asked.

'It's nothing to do with that. It has everything

to do with this little self-improvement circle.'

'I don't know what demons you are running from Ed, but they must be dark.' Louise physically turned her back towards him.

'What's that supposed to mean?'

'I won't waste my breath.'

A surge of anger washed across Ed's face and he clenched his fists. Robbie stood up, physically standing between him and Louise. Dan just stared, mouth open.

'Ed, maybe you should cut the cord,' Robbie suggested.

Ed thought for a moment before replying. 'You're not wrong. Give my love to Mr Cheung.' Ed picked up his gym bag and walked out of the pub, his face burning red with rage.

The group was silent for some time after he left.

'What was that remark about a text message?' Robbie asked.

'Ah, it was no big deal. Ed sent me a text at the weekend. I never got around to replying. He might have been a bit annoyed by that.'

Robbie held eye contact, knowingly, but did not say anything.

'You wouldn't get that amount of drama in the Abbey Theatre.' It was Dan's turn to try to lighten the mood.

'Are you okay, Louise?' Robbie asked, ignoring Dan.

'Yeah, I'm grand. Or at least I will be.'

'Do you want another drink?'

'No, not really. If I started drinking now I might never stop. Look, thanks, to both of you. I'm going to head on. We've only one class left. I don't know whether to be glad or sad. Catch up with you guys next Tuesday. Goodnight.'

When Louise had gone Dan commented, 'Ed is a complete jerk.'

'Yeah, you're right. But he's also confused. He's struggled all along with this stuff.'

'And we haven't?'

'Dan, it's like Louise said, some people are coming from a darker place.'

'What are you basing that on?'

'His behaviour, his whole attitude really. Hey, it's late. We're tired. Let's catch up again next week.'

Dan's Notebook 6

Diligent as ever, the following morning Dan captured the key points emerging from the session and the discussion which had followed:

Chapter 6

6.1 How will I get there? _Make a concrete plan to move towards your goal. It may not be all 'big stuff'. It could be a series of small incremental steps with one thing in common; they are all taking you 'North' (assuming you know which direction North is; this will fall into place if you've answered the earlier questions)._

6.2 Check your progress: _You need milestones to check progress. A weekly weigh-in, a particular amount of time spent with the kids, three hours' study per week etc. Make your plan and monitor progress against this. The formula is simple (all it needs is the willpower to see it through). Be honest with yourself._

6.3 Set the bar high or low: _Thinking big is good. But incremental steps are also good. Decide what works best for you. Some people set an enormous task for themselves and 'give up' if they don't make it. Some people find it easier to start off lifting lighter weights. It's your call._

The Final Class

The last class was a gentle re-run of the exercises that Mr Cheung had demonstrated throughout the course. Preliminary warm-ups were followed by extended stretching and the surprisingly difficult balance exercises. They followed with energetic dance movements.

The emphasis was on free-form expression. Mr Cheung teamed up opposite Dan (who was *definitely* not related to Michael Flatley) and their partnership was hilarious. Robbie was laughing so hard he had to stand off to one side.

Louise, easily the best dancer in the group, seemed to have found a particular groove tonight. She moved in time with the Latin beat, anticipating and responding to the upbeat music. Great exercise and great fun. The time went quickly. At the end of the class the trio sat around the walls in their customary position, tired but upbeat.

Mr Cheung held eye contact with Louise, Robbie and Dan in turn. He noticed, but did not comment on, Ed's absence.

'We all on journey to improve self. What happened in past we cannot control. Only control future. My father in China dead now. One time he history professor in university. During cultural revolution, many academics denounced as bourgeois. He spend time forced labour in countryside, being re-cleansed. All property taken. Last more than eight years. Father never lost hope – that future be better. He never lose idea of being "in charge" of own feelings. Some people prisoners of past which they not control or prisoners of future which they fear. Need to take control. You decide who you are. You decide what you want. You decide how get there.'

He seemed momentarily lost, distracted by a distant memory, before regaining composure. 'This journey very powerful. It lead to self-confidence and happiness. The journey never end.' He smiled.

'I also struggle long time with taking control. You best class I ever have. Work hard. Funny group. Meet to talk about big issues. You already making better tomorrow.'

Mr Cheung stood up and gave an elaborate martial arts bow. 'If you enjoy classes, please tell friends.' Inwardly, he shuddered: *Casino never lose, I need the money.* He smiled warmly, shook hands with each of them, and left.

Executive Fitness: The Juice Bar Was Hopping!

'Not sure what I'll do now on Tuesdays,' Robbie said. 'It had become part of my routine. How about you, Dan?'

'I've missed too many episodes of *Coronation Street* to get back into it,' Dan joked.

'Hey, Dan, you're developing a *wicked* sense of humour. Is this an early version of the *new* Dan that's emerging?' Louise teased.

'Let's hope so. What will you do, Louise?'

'There's no problem filling the Tuesday space. What I'll do in a broader sense I'm still not sure. What's clear though is that I will do *something*. These sessions have changed me.'

'Snap! I don't quite know how it happened, but I've done more thinking about my life these last couple of weeks than I've ever done. I think I've *already* started to change.' Robbie was equally positive.

'Oh? Like what? Let's hear the good news.' Louise smiled encouragement.

'Well, one of the personal issues for me is around the work that I do. We make good money and the hours are short, but trading commodities is not exactly saving the world.'

'I thought that the big issue for you was telling your family that you're gay,' Dan blurted.

The look from Louise communicated, 'shut up Dan'.

'It's okay, Louise. Yes, Dan, that is *one* of the issues I'm working on. Is there a ceiling on issues? I didn't know that we were limited to just one.' Robbie put on a look of mock surprise.

'I suspect that most people could only really work on one issue at a time,' Louise offered matter-of-fact.

'That's probably spot on,' Robbie concurred.

'Are you going to jump ship on the commodities trading?' she probed.

'Put that into the *not sure* box for the moment.'

'Seriously Dan, what are you hoping to do when we finish up?' Louise asked the question kindly.

'I still haven't figured it out. At each session we were given pieces of a jigsaw, but the overall picture hasn't formed. Abstract thinking is not my natural strength.' He looked thoughtful. 'It would be interesting to meet up in a couple of months and see what happens.'

'You know, Dan, that's actually a neat idea,' Robbie said. 'It does two things. It will satisfy a "curiosity need"...'

'I think you really mean nosiness,' Louise interrupted and they both laughed.

'As I was saying before my Learned Friend butted in, it might also keep the heat on each of us to follow through. Do we have a quorum?'

They all thought the idea was solid and debated the timing and format. Eventually, they agreed to write a letter outlining the changes they were going to make in their lives and post these to each other. The trio agreed to meet for dinner in six months and discuss the progress made.

'That sounds like a plan.' Dan was comfortable that something definite had been concluded.

'I've an idea,' Dan offered. 'Why don't we make it a competition? Whoever changes *least* can pick up the tab for dinner.'

Louise considered the idea for a moment. 'I'm not scared of the challenge or of picking up the tab. But the real competition is with myself, not with you or Robbie. Let's split the bill.'

'Do you want a multi-vitamin drink, Louise?' Robbie asked.

'No, another tall latté. I'm done being good for one night.'

Dan's Notebook: Final Entry

Rather than wait until the next morning, Dan decided to immediately capture the ideas which had come up at the evening session. In the past two weeks he'd taken to carrying the notebook in his briefcase and looking at the issues during spare moments. As soon as he arrived home, he retrieved the briefcase from under the stairs and wrote the following:

Chapter 7

_7.1 We are all on a journey__: Self-improvement never ends. Be happy that you are making progress, but never content that you have arrived. The journey puts something positive in the future, answering the 'something to look forward to' question._

_7.2 The climb is tough__: It initially requires courage to face up to introspection. Once you've made the plan, it requires perseverance to keep going. Personal improvement is a self-disciplined journey (that's why so many people quit; most have the ability, not everyone has the 'stickability')._

_7.3 Pick key issues__: While there is no limit of issues to work on, focus on the top two or three. Otherwise, you may feel overwhelmed and give up._

_7.4 Celebrate and reward success__: Every now and again, stop and take in the view. While there may be 'more mountain' to climb, if you look back there's probably a lot of ground already covered. Reward yourself for the progress made._

Dan looked at the notes he'd written and quickly flicked back over the previous pages. *I really owe it to myself to keep going with this stuff.* It was past midnight when he climbed into bed and almost immediately fell into a deep sleep.

Letter from Robbie

13B Tavistock Green
Sandymount,
Dublin 4

Hi Dan & Louise,

This is my 'follow-up' note – as promised! Now, where to start? Over the past couple of years I've been struggling with two issues – the first one we talked about during our afterburn sessions following training. The second issue we briefly touched on during the final evening.

Living in a gay partnership: I've long been comfortable about my sexual preference (if you think I'm confused now, you should have met me as a teenager!). But ... I've struggled to openly explain this to my parents (to my father, in particular). I always put this down to wanting to shield them from any hurt. However, I think that it's actually deeper and taps into something inside me. I don't want to overdramatise the point, but this is around some form of 'rejection fear'. While, out-wardly, I have been protecting them, perhaps I have actually been protecting myself. Dan, I kept thinking about your anecdote of being lost in the zoo and feeling alone. I think that it's time for me to face up to that possibility ('I am what I am' as the song says). I will tell my folks about Alan. The decision is clear; timing still needs a bit of work.

Wanting to make a social contribution: Buying and selling commodities is soulless – but it defi-nitely pays the bills. I struggle between enjoying reasonable 'purchasing power' and doing some-thing which has a social purpose. We've locked on to a particular lifestyle which is not that easy to change. Personally I get torn between the 'war in Sudan' and the latest BMW driving machine and, to date, the car has always won. However, it's increasingly difficult to jump out of bed for the greater glory of 'increasing shareholder value'. Not sure what the answer is here but the issue is troubling and needs to be addressed. I don't have enough money to retire. Not sure that I would want to, even if I had the moola. A real conun-drum! Hopefully I will have something positive to report when we meet. In the meantime, if you get any bright ideas, drop me a note or just call (we are in the phone book).

That's all from the Sandymount jury. Looking forward to reading through your stuff.

Best wishes,
Robbie

Letter From Louise

25 Seaview Terrace
Marino
Dublin 3

Hi Guys,

First, let me start with a big thanks to both of you. The last couple of months have been hugely developmental for me and both of you have played central roles in this.

Second, is a tiny bit of an apology. We won a major construction contract at work – which is good news. I have been appointed as the on-site Project Manager. While I've done this type of work before, nothing nearly as complex at this. It's a bit scary, but I'm up for it. The downside is that I haven't made any great progress on my 'big issue'.

But I have come up with a half-decent plan.

71

As per Dan's suggestion, I'm hoping to negotiate a time-bound level of involvement. While this sounds a bit clinical, it will definitely work for me. I think that it will also work well for mam, once she gets used to the idea. And she's actually come up with an initiative all on her own. It's almost as if she sensed something was going to change. Amazing. I'll tell you more when we meet.

There is also a little bit of new news. I've gotten myself a dog, Rusty (guess his colour?). Every night we go for a stroll and 'chat'. After hearing about your routine, Robbie, I think I've caught the exercise bug. I'm trying to stay focused on the positive – that's something else I picked up from you.

One final point. I've come to the conclusion that I'm basically proud of who I am and realise that I have a really good life. Hope that does not come across as smug or arrogant! I actually find it quite comforting.

Every best wish,
Yours Sincerely,
Louise

Letter From Dan

17, Funbally Road
Blackrock, Co. Dublin

Dear Louise & Robbie,

I am glad to have this opportunity to write to you. Over the course of our Dance-Boxing classes (I've never gotten used to that name), I struggled to put Mr Cheung's ideas into a coherent framework. Some of the confusion reflected contradictions in my own life. Possibly I should have been a bit more open about this stuff when we met but it is genuinely hard for me to discuss feelings and emotions. It has always been like that.

About 12 months ago, the position of Managing Director of my company became vacant. I really wanted it and should have been the number one candidate. I know the industry well and have worked with this company for more than 12 years. After a lot of shuffling back and forth, the job was given to another guy. He's 38 and was formerly the Head of the Marketing Department. To say that this guy does not understand the pharmaceutical business would be the understatement of the millennium.

I was bitterly disappointed. After the decision was announced I spoke with the European Head of HR. It was probably the most honest – and straightforward – feedback I'd ever received. Apparently, I am well respected for my technical ability, but am seen to be less good on the people side. The really galling part is that my wife has been telling me the same thing for years but I didn't believe her! I do now. So my life goal to become MD and to 'lead the troops' was not to be. I spent several months railing against the decision – generally acting like a child whose favourite toy had been taken away.

Side by side with this, both of our daughters left home. Adrienne moved in with her boyfriend (thankfully a nice guy); Sarah went to study in a UK university. I suppose I should be glad that they've become independent adults – but my immediate reaction was sadness. They just don't seem to need us much. So it was like the death of ambition and the end of my family life taking place at the same time. It's thrown up a lot of stuff for me – about getting old, about my career plateauing, how my wife and myself will cope when there is only two of us at home. She's smarter than me and knew instinctively that the classes would be a good idea. That's how I was 'signed up'.

I wish I was able to tell you what the answer is ... but I'm not there yet. I'm a slow-burn type and will have to wrestle with the questions for a bit longer. I think you both know that already!

I'm looking forward to catching up in a couple of months to see how you are getting on. Based on our interactions to date, I have no doubt that you will continue to be successful. I've really enjoyed the time we've spent together. I feel I've made two great new friends.

Respectfully,
Dan

P.S. I pulled together the 'minutes' of our meetings with Mr Cheung. These are attached for your interest. You see, eventually, the penny drops!

Chapter 1

<u>1.1 You are the Chief Executive (CEO) of your own life</u>: If your life is happy you've made it so. If your life is unhappy, you're also responsible (by putting up with it). While 'bad things' might happen, you need to dictate how you respond to these. If you decide not to change, then someone or something else is essentially the CEO of your life. And, you've appointed them into the position!

<u>1.2 The 'button for change' is on the inside</u>: No one can force you to change. They can advise, criticise or cajole you — but only you can decide to change. You change either because the 'pain' (today's picture) is intolerable and pushes you to do something about it, or the 'prize' (tomorrow's picture) is emotionally compelling and pulls you forward. Without a clear pain or prize, personal change goes to the bottom of the in-tray. Nothing happens.

Chapter 2

2.1 What is it you want? What would a 'better tomorrow' look like? What would the key elements be? Don't be constrained by thinking about what exists today; tomorrow could be radically different. Dare to dream about a better space. Think big thoughts.

2.2 How much do you want it? Personal change is possible – if you want it badly enough to do something about it, i.e. if the gain outweighs the pain. Do you want it enough to take on the challenge of changing your life? Ask yourself: What would I like to change about myself or my life?

2.3 Make your desires 'graphic': Make the tomorrow picture easier to see by 'chunking' it into components, making each piece as graphic as possible.

- Wealth/financial status
- Family
- Career success
- Health
- Social contribution
- Leisure time

2.4 Pleasure vs happiness: One is a short-term feeling of elation; the other is a slower burn, but provides deeper contentment. Chasing pleasure is not the route to happiness – they are often opposites. Happiness is more often a 'by-product' – you encounter it when doing something else which is important or worthwhile. It is like a shadow. If you chase after it directly – it seems to move away.

Chapter 3

3.1 _Stopping you laughing_: What is it that stops you laughing? What holds you back? Is it something, i.e. the fear of looking foolish, or someone, i.e. a particular person? If you seemed happier at one point in your life, what changed? Understanding this is a clue to what you really enjoy.

3.2 _Philosophy of happiness_: Do you have something to do, someone to love and something to look forward to? What areas of your life mean the most to you? What issues need most attention? While there are always 'lots of things' to change – one or two of these could make a real breakthrough for you. What are they?

Chapter 4

4.1 What do you stand for? Is there one central purpose in your life – one 'big idea?' Maybe there's more than one. What are these key concepts which you firmly believe in? What is it that you are here to do, your personal mission? How do you want to be remembered? How will you make a difference?

4.2 Where did it originate? Did your 'big idea' come from your family/upbringing? Did it develop because of a significant emotional experience? What is the drive/the payoff? How will life be better for you if you achieve this purpose?

4.3 Life is not fair: Not everyone is born with equal gifts. Some have great physical assets; others don't. Some people have terrific parents and supportive families; others don't. Sometimes terrible things happen – seemingly at random – which could not in any sense be described as fair. You need to 'surrender' to the idea that life is not fair, rather than keep railing against it. There is no sense that the route forward will always be linear; you may go backwards. But even when it is unfair, you remain the Chief Executive of your own life. You own your response to whatever happens.

Chapter 5

5.1 Being in control: *Are you taking control of your own life? Are you making-it-happen or saying 'what happened'? Are you secretly taking comfort in allowing someone else to lead your life or using this as an 'escape clause' for regrets or disappointments? The good news is you can be in control. The bad news is once you accept this, you can't outsource the blame.*

5.2 Stepping up to the line: *If you take on a leadership responsibility, and subsequently fail, there will be no one to blame. But, what is the opposite? Do you want to spend your life following someone else's agenda? You own the responsibility to make your own life a success (however you define this). It can be different (if you want it to be). What stops most people is the fear of failure – when the only real failure is not trying.*

Chapter 6

6.1 How will I get there? Make a concrete plan to move towards your goal. It may not be all 'big stuff'. It could be a series of small incremental steps with one thing in common; they are all taking you 'North' (assuming you know which direction North is; this will fall into place if you've answered the earlier questions).

6.2 Check your progress: You need milestones to check progress. A weekly weigh-in, a particular amount of time spent with the kids, three hours' study per week etc. Make your plan and monitor progress against this. The formula is simple (all it needs is the willpower to see it through). Be honest with yourself.

6.3 Set the bar high or low: Thinking big is good. But incremental steps are also good. Decide what works best for you. Some people set an enormous task for themselves and 'give up' if they don't make it. Some people find it easier to start off lifting lighter weights. It's your call.

Chapter 7

7.1 We are all on a journey: *Self-improvement never ends. Be happy that you are making progress, but never content that you have arrived. The journey puts something positive in the future, answering the 'something to look forward to' question.*

7.2 The climb is tough: *It initially requires courage to face up to introspection. Once you've made the plan, it requires perseverance to keep going. Personal improvement is a self-disciplined journey (that's why so many people quit; most have the ability, not everyone has the 'stickability').*

7.3 Pick key issues: *While there is no limit of issues to work on, focus on the top two or three. Otherwise, you may feel overwhelmed and give up.*

7.4 Celebrate and reward success: *Every now and again, stop and take in the view. While there may be 'more mountain' to climb, if you look back there's probably a lot of ground already covered. Reward yourself for the progress made.*

Facing up to the Awkward Conversation

The traffic on the M50 was particularly slow. Robbie was frustrated as his car inched along the motorway. Even after he'd cleared the Red Cow roundabout (known in Dublin as the 'Mad Cow' roundabout), a long, boring drive to County Clare lay ahead. He switched radio channels irritably, searching for familiar music. It would take almost four hours to get to his parents' home.

Robbie greeted his mother, answering her questions about the latest happenings in work – including an update on where and what he ate each day. It was their standard food debate – solidly comforting. He was putting off the awkward moment for as long as possible.

'Dad, I need a word with you. There's something we need to discuss.'

'Yes, Robert, no problem.' His father always used his full name.

'We could walk over as far as the headland.'

'Sure, it's like a summer's day today, so it is. That's a grand idea.'

'Okay, let's do the walk.'

The three-mile round-trip was about an hour's walk at a leisurely pace. For the first time Robbie noticed his father's movements slowing and he deliberately took a lighter pace. They didn't speak at all for the first mile or so.

'Dad, I've something to tell you. Eh ... it's a bit awkward.'

'There's nothing awkward for us. Go ahead son.'

'Okay, well you know my friend Alan?'

'I do indeed.'

'Well ... we are actually more than just friends.'

'Sure, don't you share that apartment in Dublin. You two are always out on the tear. Your mother worries about you – the stress of the job, whether you get enough sleep and all that exercise too. She thinks you're overdoing it, so she does.'

Robbie was not sure whether his Dad was missing the message or was deliberately being evasive.

'Dad, Alan and I are partners. We live together.'

'But that might all change if you meet someone. Before I met your mother sure I was wild myself. Too much drinking, that's for sure. But, she sorted me out in jig-time.'

'Dad, I'm not looking to meet someone. I already *have* met someone. It's Alan.'

They walked in silence for a quarter of a mile.

'Robert, look out there, beyond that outcrop of rocks. When you were a little fella, I used to tell you that if we dived in there we could swim west all the way to America. Do you remember?'

'Vaguely.'

'Oh, we spent some hours there looking for crabs in the rock pools and kicking ball on the beach. You practically grew up with a football in your hands.'

'Dad, did you hear what I said earlier?'

'You know, being here again brings back all of those memories. The good times come flooding back. Come on son, your mother will think we've sneaked down to O'Neill's for a pint. We'd best be getting home. The light has completely fallen in on us.'

They didn't speak at all on the final walk towards home.

Six Months Later: The Reunion Night

Robbie had taken on the job of organising the rendezvous. He wanted a restaurant that was smart enough for the occasion – but not overly pretentious. Roly's in Ballsbridge was chosen. Good food and excellent service, it would be bang on for their purpose.

Dan arrived first, in a suit and tie, a tad formal for the occasion. Robbie wore his trademark smart casuals – managing to create a combined air of fitness and confidence. Louise had definitely lost weight and looked sun-tanned and healthy. The conversation, after an interruption of several months, started off slowly.

'See anything you like on the menu?' Robbie asked.

'I like all of it,' Louise said.

'This place is a bit more expensive than I remember it.' Robbie was conscious that he'd chosen the venue.

'Don't worry. It's cheaper than psychiatry,' Louise quipped. 'How have you been?'

'Fine,' from Dan.

'Good, very good. No problems.' Louise seemed a little subdued.

'Okay, let's get the ordering out the way. Maybe a bottle of, say, Chateauneuf du Pape, to loosen up. Agreed?'

'Anything as long as it's red. You seem in good form Robbie, and you look great.'

'I am in good form, thanks.'

They had been in the restaurant all of five minutes when Dan asked directly: 'Well, I suppose we have to get started on this feedback. How is your relationship with your mother?'

Louise smiled fondly at Dan. 'It's a good story. Every Sunday we plan something, usually we go somewhere. The place is not important, being together is. Three weeks ago we went to the Municipal Art Gallery. There is a bit of 'previous' here. My mother *hates* art galleries.' Louise made a shock-horror gesture and laughed loud enough to bring disapproving stares from the couple seated at the next table.

'You mentioned in your letter that something else happened with your mother, some initiative. What was that all about?' Robbie asked.

'Oh yes, I'd almost forgotten. She joined a ladies club. To be honest, I was floored. Mam met a woman in the supermarket, someone she knew from years ago. The other lady encouraged her to come down and "bingo"!'

'They play bingo?' Dan asked.

'No, Dan. It's a figure of speech. I meant "bingo", it all knitted into place.' Louise tried to suppress a giggle.

'It's working out?'

'Better than that, Robbie. Mam has managed to regain her independence and I've retrieved some of my own space. But, you know, it's more than just a *time management* success. When I'm with her now, I enjoy rather than resent the time. While she is still lonely, it just doesn't seem to come up as often. It's great.'

'That *is* a good story,' Dan offered.

'It's a *great* story and a lot of it is down to those classes we did.'

'And how is the dog doing?' Robbie asked.

'Rusty is my silent therapist. Every night he gets a project update and never goes into bad humour, even when I'm miles over budget. He's such a great listener.'

'Yeah. Unconditional positive regard. That's what you're supposed to get from human therapists. I must have read that somewhere.' Robbie seemed to know a lot about therapy and positive psychology, but Louise didn't pursue the point. No forced confession was the silent rule.

'What type of dog is he?' Dan asked.

'A Heinz. Fifty-seven varieties. He picked me out when I visited the dog pound.'

'And you have the time to manage him?'

'During the week it's tight. We do a quick "around the block". At the weekend I bring him on a longer jaunt. Even my Mother likes Rusty.'

'What prompted *that* decision?' Robbie asked.

'Well, we always had a dog when I was growing up. I just like dogs, that's all.'

'And?' Robbie sensed there was something more.

'I dunno. Maybe secretly I wanted to address

Mr Cheung's *someone to love idea*. Rusty is the only man in my life – for the moment. Anyway, enough about me. What are you up to, Dan?'

'I'm fine. In better shape than the last time we spoke.'

'What's happened?'

'A couple of things have fallen into place. Nothing particularly earth-shattering. But together, they've made a difference. A real difference.'

The starters, ordered earlier, arrived and disrupted the flow of the conversation.

'Like what?' Robbie asked when they resumed.

'Well, I plucked up the courage to have a conversation with my new boss. I apologised for being a jerk and resenting his success. I have to say he was very gracious about it. What emerged was that they really do see my technical expertise as an asset. I thought they were just blowing me off. I've now started working on a European-wide quality control protocol for the business, side-by-side with my day job. It's *genuinely* interesting.'

'Do you have to travel a lot?' Louise quizzed.

'Not a huge amount. The worst part is getting through Dublin Airport.'

They nodded in agreement.

'Anyway, with the job more or less sorted, I've

been able to focus on the family. We helped one daughter move all her stuff to Edinburgh University and get settled. Apart from complaints about the weather, she's grand. My other daughter has just bought a second-hand house with her partner. It needs a lot of work, so, I'll be busy for the next while, DIY-ing.' Dan smiled at his own joke.

'You sound good about it,' Robbie said.

'This is the most contented I've felt for a long time. It's impossible to put a number on it, but I probably feel 90 per cent better than I did before.'

'Your wife must have noticed a change.'

'She has, Louise. Everyone has.'

Dan was more vocal than they'd ever seen him.

'I can't believe how well you captured the central ideas in the "minutes". Where did you get all that supplementary stuff?' Robbie seemed genuinely impressed.

'It's the CASE philosophy.'

'What's that?'

'Copy and steal everything. There's a bookshop in Nassau Street with tons of self-help stuff. I think I'm their best customer. I was always good at writing – once I have a bit of time to digest the ideas.'

'It was brilliant to have all of the stuff in a single place. It's sort of become a reference manual for living. And I *do* refer to it.' Louise lifted her glass in a salute to Dan.

The main courses arrived, beautifully presented.

'What about you, Robbie? Bring us up-to-date.'

'We seem to have caught each other on a good night. There were two dilemmas for me. Coming out to my family and finding a job which had more of a social contribution.'

'You described them really well in your note,' Louise commented.

'It's amazing how clear the issues were framed after we'd gone through the questions suggested by Mr Cheung.'

'Did you tell your family?' Dan asked.

Robbie smiled. 'Yes, Dan, I did.'

'And?'

'Well, it turned out my mother had known all along. It had simply become undiscussable. In a weird way, she did not want to bring it up for fear of embarrassing *me*. Can you believe that? It reminded me of the old Mark Twain quip, "I have been through terrible things in my life, some of which actually happened".' It was vintage Robbie, thoughtful and funny.

'Was everyone equally okay with it?' Louise asked. 'How did your dad react?'

'He's conservative. I know it's not what he would have chosen. But ... now that we have gotten over the *telling phase*, our relationship might move into a better space. Next week they are coming to stay with me in Dublin. But Alan is going to move out of the apartment. They're not really ready yet.'

'Are you disappointed ...?' Louise left the question unfinished.

'I'm glad we broached the issue. It was really awkward and it's not resolved by any means. Maybe it never will be. But the genie is out of the bottle now and that itself is satisfying.' Louise sensed that there was something more. *Maybe another time. No forced confessions.*

'What did you do in relation to the job? The social contribution idea,' Dan asked pointedly.

'Ah! That one has been a bit easier. I was caught between two contradictory ideas.'

'Smoked Salmon Socialism,' Dan offered.

'You've gone all cryptic on us again. What does that mean?' Robbie asked.

'Probably before your time. It was a term used to describe some senior members of the Labour Party – who were supposedly torn between the ideals of socialism and the attractions of the good life,' Dan replied. 'I don't think it was a real dilemma at all. Just a phrase constructed by some political spin doctor to nobble the left-wing op-position.' He smiled.

'You know Dan, sometimes you have piercing insight. It's lying there, waiting, and every now and then it just bursts out.'

'Go on with the story,' Dan said, slightly embarrassed, but pleased by the attention.

'Okay, I've been wrestling with this contradiction. We have a particular lifestyle and it's hard to roll back on that. So ... I've decided to stay in the business for another eight years – until I'm 50 – and reconsider my options at that time. In the meantime I'm going to give 10 per cent of my net income to two charities that work with kids – one in Ireland and one in a South African township just outside Capetown.'

'What a great thing to do,' Louise said. She was silent for a moment, before adding: 'Will it satisfy the need?'

'Time will tell but I'm happy with the concept. It's a good fit with my lifestyle, with where everything is right now.'

'How did you come up with *that* solution?' Dan asked.

'I'm not really sure. The origin of individual ideas is a bit unclear. Did you find that? Anyway, who cares?'

'You seem happy, Robbie,' Louise observed.

'Happy doesn't describe it. I'm delighted with where I am right now. Think about it. I was faced with two dilemmas. Now both issues have at least been addressed. Somehow, I seem to have made "peace with imperfection". Do you remember that line?'

'I think we all sort of feel the same.'

There was a moment of calm, satisfied reflection.

'On the subject of imperfection, I wonder what Ed is up to tonight.' Robbie said.

Louise bristled at the comment.

'That's unfair. Ed just struggled a bit more than the rest of us.'

'Maybe.'

'You don't buy that?'

'Eh ... somewhere deep down I probably do. It's just that he wasn't easy to be around.'

'Yeah, he wasn't terrific company like the rest of us.' Dan held a straight face for as long as he could and then started grinning. They all laughed.

'Ed was in de-nial – and that's *not* the longest river in Africa,' Robbie quipped.

Dan laughed at the joke but Louise seemed uncomfortable. 'Denial is an okay place. Sometimes the truth is too painful to confront.'

'I think you're wrong, Louise. If you don't confront whatever is facing you, you effectively take a decision to stay in the same place. Ed just wanted to outsource the blame. He could have a master's degree in excuse making. Do you remember the Eleanor Roosevelt line? She said, "No one can make you feel inferior without your consent". Ed needs to face up to his issues – demons and all.' It was stated forcefully – but not harshly.

'Look, I'm not defending Ed. I *probably* even agree with you. I just feel a bit awkward talking about him when he's not here. That's all.'

'One of the self-help books I read made the point that winners and losers are both self-determined. But only winners acknowledge it.' Robbie, in trademark fashion, was not letting the argument die. They were silent for a moment.

'Hey, getting back to us, do you think this mini-euphoria will last?' Dan asked, skilfully changing the topic.

'Unfortunately, the shelf-life for happiness tends to be short. It's almost the human condition to soak up what's good and look for the next thing,' Robbie said. 'What do you think, Louise?'

'Each of us has, somehow, come to a better place. The skills we've acquired, in confronting the things which bothered us, should hold up pretty well.'

'With Mr Cheung's "big questions" and Dan's diary to dip into, I certainly feel equipped to face the future,' she added.

'Then maybe it's an appropriate time to suggest a toast.'

Robbie raised his glass. 'To the future.'

'To the future', Louise and Dan repeated as they clinked glasses and then savoured the subtle flavours of the French wine.

Epilogue

Ed is still working hard. The kids are getting a bit older and slightly easier to manage. Sometime after abandoning the fitness classes, Ed had a relationship with a younger woman in the sales department, but it's since fizzled out. He hopes to go back to college at some point – when the timing is right. He's still not entirely comfortable with his current job or his ability to provide financial security to his wife and kids (getting rich is a brutally slow process). Some people definitely seem to be luckier, getting easy money through inheritance or being 'in the know' job-wise. Coming from a modest income family, Ed sometimes jokingly refers to himself as having been born with a 'rusty spoon' in his mouth. He keeps buying lotto tickets and is hoping that 'it could be him'.

Mr Cheung continues to run Executive Fitness – combining 'flexercise' classes with executive coaching in his own unique style. On a personal basis he found it impossible to give up gambling completely

– but now limits his betting to €150 a week. It's a compromise, but one that he is comfortable with. He's recently taken up playing golf – bringing his trademark passion and dedication to perfecting his swing technique. It's a lifetime goal.

About the Author

D r. Paul Mooney was appointed President of the National College of Ireland in 2007. Paul holds a Ph.D (Industrial Sociology) and a Graduate Diploma in Industrial Relations from Trinity College, Dublin and a National Diploma in Industrial Relations from the National College of Ireland. He is a Fellow of the Chartered Institute of Personnel and Development.

He began his career as a tradesman, subsequently moving into production management. He later joined General Electric where, over six years, he held a number of increasingly responsible human resource positions.

After GE Paul worked with Sterling Drug in Ireland. Subsequently, as Human Resource Director for the Pacific Rim, he had responsibility for all personnel activity in South East Asia.

In 1991, Paul established PMA Consulting, a boutique management consulting company which ran Organisation and Management Development programmes.

Paul is the author of eight books: *Amie, the True Story of Adoption in Asia* (1990), *Developing the High Performance Organisation* (1996), *The Effective Consultant: How to Develop the High Performance Organisation* (1999), *Keeping Your Best Staff: The Human Resources Challenge in a Competitive Environment* (1999), *Turbo Charging the HR Function* (2001), *The Badger Ruse* (2004) – a crime thriller set in Dublin – and *Union-Free: Creating a Committed, Productive Workforce* (2005). He has also published a range of articles on effective organisation and people management.